W9-AUI-731

HARRIET TUBMAN

and the Underground Railroad

Dan Stearns

WORLD ALMANAC® LIBRARY

Please visit our web site at: www.worldalmanaclibrary.com
For a free color catalog describing World Almanac® Library's list of high-quality books
and multimedia programs, call 1-800-848-2928 (USA) or 1-800-387-3178 (Canada).
World Almanac® Library's fax: (414) 332-3567.

Library of Congress Cataloging-in-Publication Data

Stearns, Dan.
    Harriet Tubman and the Underground Railroad / Dan Stearns.
        p. cm. — (In the footsteps of American heroes)
    Includes bibliographical references and index.
    ISBN 0-8368-6428-X (lib. bdg.)
    ISBN 0-8368-6433-6 (softcover)
        1. Tubman Harriet (1820?-1913)—Juvenile literature. 2. Underground railroad—
Juvenile literature. 3. Slaves—United States—Biography—Juvenile literature.
    4. African American women—Biography—Juvenile literature. I. Title. II. Series.
E444.T82S74   2006
973.7'115092—dc22
[B]   2005054474

First published in 2006 by
World Almanac® Library
A Member of the WRC Media Family of Companies
330 West Olive Street, Suite 100
Milwaukee, WI 53212 USA

Produced by Compendium Publishing Ltd
First Floor, 43 Frith Street
London W1D 4SA

For Compendium Publishing
Editors: Don Gulbrandsen and Joe Hollander
Picture research: Mindy Day and Sandra Forty
Design: Ian Hughes/Compendium Design
Artwork: Mark Franklin

World Almanac® Library managing editor: Valerie J. Weber
World Almanac® Library editor: Leifa Butrick
World Almanac® Library art direction: Tammy West
World Almanac® Library production: Jessica Morris and Robert Kraus

Photo Credits: Library of Congress: cover, chapter openers, and all except as indicated; Corbis:
pages 15(both), 16, 17(both), 22, 27(both), 32, 34(T), 37, 39, 40(both), 41(all), 52, 53, 57, 59;
Getty Images: 18, 29(t), 30, 33, 34(b), 35(both), 55(both)

Printed in the United States of America

1 2 3 4 5 6 7 8 9 10 09 08 07 06

CONTENTS

COVER AND TITLE PAGE: This image—also used as part of each chapter opening—is a photograph of Harriet Tubman taken in 1880. By this time, she had led many slaves along the Underground Railroad to safety, spied for the Union Army, nursed soldiers, and worked to help former slaves gain new lives.

INTRODUCTION

Imagine you hear the sounds of men shouting and dogs barking somewhere behind you. It is night, and you are hiding in the woods, praying that no one sees you. You are breathing hard; you have been running, fleeing the frightening sounds in the distance and all they represent. You are a human being, but you are being hunted because you are a slave.

Your life as a slave is filled with hard work and harsh punishments. Everything you are and everything you do belongs to someone else. You have no control over the present, and you very likely have no future. All your decisions are made for you, and none of them are pleasant.

Back in the woods, you try to calm yourself as the angry voices and barking dogs come steadily closer. You see an opening ahead of you in the dark—a trail that heads north. This is what you have been seeking. You have been told that this trail is the key to escaping from your life as a slave. It will be a tough trip, filled with danger, and you might be pursued by slave catchers every step of the way, but if you make it to the end of this trail, nobody can ever say they own you again. You breathe deeply, step out of your hiding place, and take a courageous first step on the trail—your journey on the Underground Railroad.

The concept of slavery—of one human being owning another human being as property—is unthinkable today. Yet slavery was an important institution in the United States during the country's early history. The first Africans arrived in Virginia in 1619 as indentured servants, and colonists quickly discovered their value as unpaid laborers. Soon the colonies legalized slavery, and a profitable—yet horrible—trade in African slaves developed. Over time, the

The Underground Railroad by Charles T. Webber, dating from around 1893. The Underground Railroad is the metaphor used to describe the route and the method used to help fugitive African Americans escape from slavery. The word *Underground* doesn't mean that there were tunnels involved, and the word *Railroad* doesn't mean that there were engines and train cars. It was underground in the sense that it was secret, and it was a railroad because there were regularly used routes.

Southern states developed farm economies that were almost totally dependent on African American slaves who worked in the fields growing and harvesting tobacco, cotton, rice, and other cash crops on large plantations.

In the industrial North, slavery was not important to the economy. Many Northerners thought it was wrong. Northern states made the practice illegal within their own boundaries between 1789 and 1830. Importing new slaves into the United States became illegal in 1807. The abolitionist movement to end slavery throughout all the states gained momentum. Ultimately, the conflict over states' rights to make decisions about slavery and over the morality of slavery itself led to the Civil War. This bloody conflict killed more than one-half million soldiers and for a time broke the United States into two nations.

The decades preceding the war were a difficult time for slaves, who had no control over their existence and faced lives of backbreaking labor. They could marry and start families, only to have their spouses and children sold and taken away from them forever. Their owners fed and clothed them, but they could punish them mercilessly for the tiniest infraction. Slaves lived hard, short lives; fewer than four out of any one hundred slaves lived to age sixty.

Despite their difficult lives, slaves lived with the knowledge that freedom was a possibility for them.

Not all black people were slaves. Some were freed by their owners, and some even purchased their freedom. They knew that if they lived in the North or in Canada, they would be free because slavery in those places was illegal. Out of this knowledge came a dream that later became a reality: It was possible to escape to freedom by traveling the Underground Railroad.

The Underground Railroad was not a real railroad with tracks and trains. It was a secret network of trails that operated a little like a railroad. The system had its own stations (buildings where trains or escaping slaves stopped and rested), conductors (the "boss" of a train, or the person in charge of a group of escaping slaves), and junctions

A large group of slaves standing in front of buildings on Smith's Plantation, Beaufort, South Carolina

Reproduction of an 1860 broadside. It was a typical advertisement of the times, offering a reward for fugitive slaves.

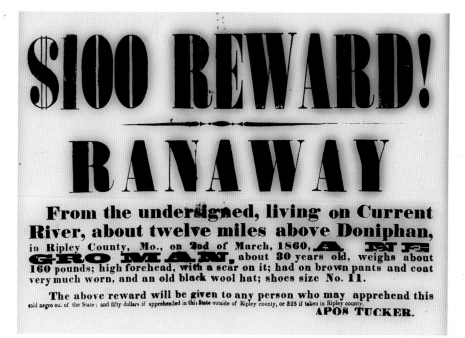

$100 REWARD!

RANAWAY

From the undersigned, living on Current River, about twelve miles above Doniphan, in Ripley County, Mo., on 2nd of March, 1860, A NEGRO MAN, about 30 years old, weighs about 160 pounds; high forehead, with a scar on it; had on brown pants and coat very much worn, and an old black wool hat; shoes size No. 11.

The above reward will be given to any person who may apprehend this said negro out of the State; and fifty dollars if apprehended in this State outside of Ripley county, or $25 if taken in Ripley county.

APOS TUCKER.

(places where tracks—or escape trails—crossed). Slaves from the Southern states could travel along this secret network and escape to freedom in the North and Canada. The Underground Railroad resulted from the hard work of abolitionists, including black and white families, churches, and individuals opposed to slavery. In the decades before the Civil War, they set up "safe houses" for escaped slaves that eventually evolved into the organized network that became the Underground Railroad.

Many people worked on the Underground Railroad to help escaping slaves. However, one unique woman emerged from this era whose love of freedom, courage, and concern for others makes her an inspiration for people today: Harriet Tubman.

Harriet was born into slavery but dreamed of being free. Eventually, she escaped to the North, but just getting away from slavery was not enough for this special woman. She wanted to share freedom with other people. So, in the years before the Civil War, she became one of the leading conductors for the Underground Railroad. After making her own escape, she made thirteen trips into the South to lead escaping slaves to freedom. During the war, she was a nurse and a spy for the North. She even led troops on a successful raid in South Carolina. After the war, she continued fighting for people who needed someone to speak up for them: newly freed black children deserving an education, women struggling to win the right to vote, the poor and elderly without a decent place to live.

This book will follow a trail that includes the Underground Railroad and a great deal of Harriet Tubman's life. This journey through time will explore some of the other key players, events, and places that were all part of this fascinating story. By the end, it will be clear that by never giving up on a dream, one person can change the lives of many other people—and even change how his or her country behaves towards its citizens.

Harriet Tubman's journey can be followed on this map and the one on pages 58–59. The green dots represent the places mentioned on the sidebars. The red dots represent important places of interest in the history of the Underground Railroad. The addresses, Web sites and telephone numbers of all the numbered sites are listed in Places to Visit and Research on pages 56–57.

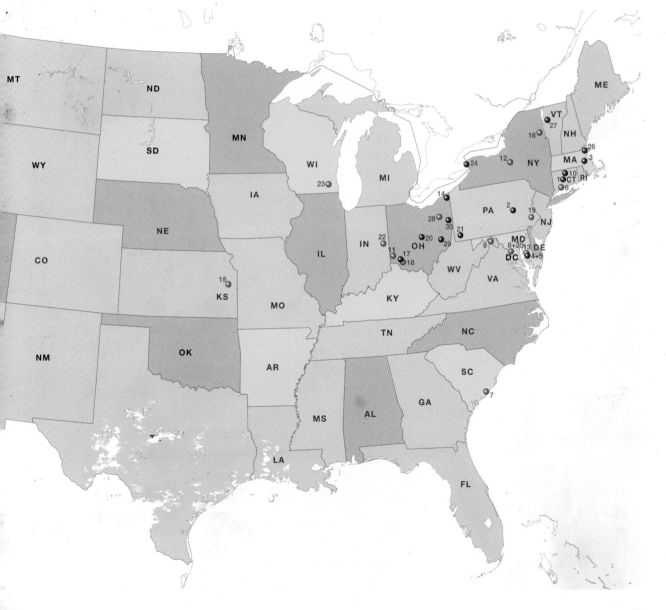

CHAPTER 1
HARRIET TUBMAN'S EARLY LIFE

The United States was still a very young nation in 1820, at the time of Harriet Tubman's birth. (The exact date is uncertain, but most scholars place Tubman's birthday between 1820 and 1825.) The Constitution had been ratified only thirty years earlier, and no one expected a Civil War to divide the country.

Slavery in the South was a way of life, and at that time, most Southerners probably believed that slavery would always be around. Even in those days, however, a web of routes, leading out of the South toward the Northern U.S. states and Canada, was beginning to make a difference.

Tubman's first home was on the eastern shore of Chesapeake Bay in Maryland, a land of grain fields, marshes, woods, and rivers. The Edward Brodess farm near Bucktown, where Harriet and her family lived, was not large by plantation standards, but it still used slaves to work the land.

Her mother's name was Harriet "Rit" Green, and her father was Benjamin Ross. Tubman's name at birth was Araminta "Minty" Ross. Tubman's mother was a strong woman and probably a great influence on young Harriet. When Harriet was twelve, a slave trader from Georgia attempted to purchase Harriet's brother Moses. For many slaves, "Georgia" could mean anywhere in the Deep South. Because of the hard work on cotton fields, and the greater distance to possible freedom in the North, no slave wanted to be sold down to Georgia.

Rather than turn Moses over to the slave trader, Tubman's mother hid him for two months, not giving in to the demands of Brodess (her master) or the appeals of the Georgia broker. The trader stuck around for a while—it was normal for slave traders to stay in a region for some time, making purchases—until Brodess simply told him to forget about it and refunded the money. This event probably made a huge impression on young Harriet.

As a slave, Harriet had a difficult childhood. In later life, she recalled putting on layers and layers of clothing as padding because her mistresses would hit her every morning. On one occasion, she bit her master's knee. The whippings stopped after that.

When Harriet was five, a nearby family paid her owner to let her come work for them. She had to do domestic work—cleaning, bringing in firewood, and even taking care of the new master and mistress's infant. Harriet was still so little at the time, she had to sit on the floor to make sure the baby would not slip out of her hands.

After working all day, young Harriet had to stay up most of the night, too. If the baby cried and woke up her master and mistress, Harriet was punished. She once said that she was whipped five times before breakfast while working at this house.

As Harriet grew older, she also grew out of domestic chores and was hired out as a field worker. Then, at the age of twelve, she suffered severe injuries that would affect her for the rest of her life.

Heading over to a local store to purchase kitchen supplies for the plantation cook, she found out that her overseer was going to punish one of the young men for leaving the fields. Because the young field hand was going to the store as well, she tried to run ahead and warn him. Harriet stood in the doorway of the store while the frightened young man fled. The slave owner meant to punish him and threw a heavy lead weight in his direction. Although it was probably an accident, the weight struck Harriet on the head instead.

Harriet spent the next two days unable to move. Weeks and months went by, with Harriet slipping into deep sleep, then waking, then falling into deep sleep again. Finally, Harriet seemed to recover, although for the rest of her life, she would occasionally slip into what she called "spells"— episodes where she blacked out. In later years, she was

HARRIET'S EARLY LIFE IN DORCHESTER COUNTY

Modern-day Dorchester County, Maryland, provides some excellent opportunities to explore the world of Harriet Tubman's early life. The Harriet Tubman Museum & Learning Center (map reference 13) in Cambridge, Maryland, is a good place to start. A historical marker notes the site of the Brodess Plantation near Cambridge where Harriet was born. The site of Bazzel Church, where her family worshiped lies 1 mile (0.6 kilometers) south on Bestpitch Ferry Road. Harriet grew up near Bucktown. The store in this village is where she received a blow to her head when an overseer tried to stop a disobedient slave. The current owners of the store invite visitors to call or stop by.

even known to have a blackout in midsentence, wake up later, and continue what she was saying as though nothing had happened. Today, this condition is known as narcolepsy.

Marriage and Dreams of Freedom

In 1840, Ben Ross, Harriet's father, was granted his freedom. His owner, Anthony Thompson, had died in 1836, and a provision in his will set Ben free. Ben was forty-five years old, and his everyday life probably did not change that much at first. He worked the same land and lived in the same place. After all, his wife and children remained slaves, and he wanted to remain near them.

Harriet did some searching into her mother's background and found out that her mother, Harriet Green, should have been freed. Harriet Green's first owner was a man by the name of Atthow Pattison. Pattison's will instructed that all of his female slaves and their children serve only until they were forty-five years old. Harriet's mother, "Rit," was now sixty.

Edward Brodess was the great-grandson of Atthow Pattison. It is possible he did not know the terms of Pattison's will. Legal wrangling by relatives after Brodess's death prevented Rit from obtaining her freedom.

In 1844, Harriet married John Tubman, a freeman. Not much is known about John Tubman, except that he and Harriet may have worked on some of the same farms. They did not have any children, but they both lived on

AM I NOT A MAN AND A BROTHER?

IN THE COTTON FIELD.

THE LASH.

Far left: In the Cotton Field. A contemporary illustration by Henry Louis Stephens (1824–1882) showing the cotton fields of the South. His picture, created in 1863, makes clear the dependence of the Southern economy on cotton and slaves.

Left: The Lash by Henry Louis Stephens, dated around 1863

Dr. Anthony Thompson's property. Thompson was a nearby landowner to whom Harriet had been hired out.

Despite the fact that they were married, Harriet and John faced very different lives. John was free and had much more security. Harriet was still a slave, and her life was very uncertain. The lure of freedom—and the fear of being sold and sent South—made Harriet realize that it might be time make a bold move.

Harriet kept hearing rumors about slaves at the Brodess plantation being sold. She prayed that God would "either change Edward Brodess' heart or bring him home, so he can't cause any more trouble." Brodess died shortly afterward. Tubman felt horribly guilty because it seemed her prayer was answered.

Edward Brodess's death left debts to settle. Because he had always owned more slaves than he could afford to keep (one of the reasons so many were hired out), the rumor around the plantation was that Harriet and two of her brothers were to be sold to new owners in the Deep South. Harriet ran away in the fall of 1849 before she could be sold—probably not knowing for certain that she would ever return.

CHAPTER 2
THE UNIVERSE OF SLAVERY

The history of slavery in North America is a long one. As long ago as the 1530s, early Spanish ships brought slaves to the New World. The first captive African workers arrived in Jamestown, the first permanent English settlement, in 1619—a whole year before the *Mayflower* landed off the coast of Massachusetts.

The conditions on slave ships were terrible. According to writings at the time, slaves were stacked "like books on a shelf," with no more than 18 inches (45 centimeters) of space between each person. A journey from Africa to North America or the Caribbean could take up to ten weeks. One of the first accounts of the overseas trip was published in 1789 by Gustavus Vassa (or Olaudah Equiano, as he is also known). He mentions the "unbearable stench" in the hold of the ship because of so many people crammed into one space. He said that if he had been able to escape the ship to a likely death by drowning, he would have. "I would have dropped over the side—but could not. Besides, the crew would watch us very closely, lest we leap into the waters."

The Debate Over Slavery

Not everyone in the New World supported buying and selling human beings. Even as early as 1688, in Germantown, Pennsylvania, a group of Quakers organized what is thought to be the earliest organized protest against slavery. By 1700, Samuel Sewall had published one of the first antislavery pamphlets, called *The Selling of Joseph*.

Slavery challenged the moral principles of Americans in many ways. In Maryland prior to 1664, slaves who became Christians could be granted freedom. But in 1664, the law was repealed, possibly in an effort to keep a ready and

Slaves using the first cotton gin. This machine separated cotton fibers from the seeds, a job previously done by hand.

An early illustration of the cotton gin

ELI WHITNEY AND THE COTTON GIN

The purpose behind Eli Whitney's cotton gin was to save labor, but only after the cotton had been planted, tended to, and harvested. Whitney's engine (shortened to the word "gin") pulled the oily seeds from cotton, making it easier and more profitable to create the 500-pound (227-kilogram) bales needed for the textile market.

In the late 1700s, the United States produced only about three thousand bales of cotton each year. By the early 1800s, only a few years after Whitney perfected his machine in 1793, the United States produced more than one hundred thousand bales. By the eve of the Civil War, annual cotton production had surged to four million bales.

Cotton was not an easy crop to grow or maintain. It needed a warm, damp climate to grow. The weather in the Deep South was perfect. Since Whitney's invention was easy to copy, cotton plantations throughout the South soon made use of the machine.

However, an expanding market for cotton demanded more land and more labor—in the form of slaves. Even though not all plantations grew cotton (the Brodess plantation, where Harriet Tubman was born, for example, did not), some historians believe that slaves may not have been in such strong demand if a cotton gin had never been invented.

Ironically, Whitney never derived much financial benefit from his invention. Even though he had a patent on the device, he was never able to protect the patent from imitators. Instead he turned his attention to making firearms. Whitney's genius proved itself again, and he developed a system of manufacturing that allowed unskilled laborers to build high-quality products and revolutionized American industry.

The Eli Whitney Museum in New Haven, Connecticut (map reference 61), is located on the site of the inventor's ground-breaking gun factory. Its programs are dedicated to preserving the Whitney legacy and to encourage the inventive spirit he championed.

cheap labor force, and the colony voted to enforce lifelong submission to slavery.

This debate was not limited to Maryland. In Virginia, similar laws went back and forth. One law said that as long as a slave was a Christian before arriving in the

A typical cotton plantation on the Mississippi. Although it was published in 1884 after the Civil War and the abolition of slavery, this illustration still helps to illustrate the world of Harriet Tubman and the economics of the South.

Iron slave shackles from Zaire as seen in the Museum of Central Africa, Terveren, Brussels, Belgium

colony, he or she could go free. Most Africans had no opportunity to learn about Christianity before they became slaves. By 1725, Virginia passed a law giving slaves the right to organize a separate Baptist church.

Of course, even in early North American history, slaves were not merely passive. Riots and rebellion were understandable reactions to unbearable conditions. In September 1739, one of the most violent slave revolts took place near Stono, South Carolina.

The Stono revolt may have started as a political maneuver incited by Spain against the British colony. At the time, the Spanish declared that they would free any slaves who could make their way to the Spanish settlement of St. Augustine, Florida. Early in the morning on September 9, about twenty slaves attacked a store and stole its guns and ammunition. The armed men marched along, killing whites when they encountered them and recruiting more slaves to go with them to St. Augustine. By early afternoon, about twenty-five white slave owners and their families were dead. Late in the day, a colonial militia attacked the slaves. Thirty slaves were killed, and the rebellion was crushed.

Slaves fought during the American Revolution as well. During the war, Vermont abolished slavery within its borders, even before it became a state. After the war, in 1783, Massachusetts abolished slavery, and all the Northern states outlawed importing slaves. In Virginia, slaves who fought in the Continental Army were granted freedom.

Nonetheless, a nationwide repeal of slavery did not occur. At the Constitutional Convention in 1787, Benjamin Franklin kept a resolution to abolish slavery to himself; he was afraid many of the other delegates would walk away. More than half of them either owned slaves or had ties to slavery. About that time, Thomas Jefferson famously compared slavery to having "a wolf by the ears. We can neither hold him, nor safely let him go."

To proslavery forces in the early republic, later slave rebellions seemed to prove him right.

The capture of Nat Turner

The Nat Turner Rebellion

Nat Turner was a slave born in Virginia on October 2, 1800. When Nat was twenty-one, he ran away from his master, Samuel Turner, and stayed hidden for a month. He returned because he felt that God had commanded him to go back.

As a young adult, Nat continued to have visions. In 1828, he felt he had been instructed by a holy spirit to "slay my [his] enemies with their own weapons." Three years later, Turner interpreted an eclipse of the sun as a sign to begin planning his revolt. In August 1831, Turner set his plan in motion.

Setting off late at night on August 21, Turner and six of his men began moving from farm to farm, killing white families, beginning at the plantation where Turner worked. By morning, Turner's force grew to about forty, and they had killed fifty-five whites.

Resistance came quickly, though. A militia tracked down Turner's men, and in the fighting that followed, many were

In *The Confessions of Nat Turner*, the leader of the insurrection tells his story to Thomas R. Grady, who recorded it.

THE

CONFESSIONS

OF

NAT TURNER,

THE LEADER

OF

THE LATE INSURRECTION

IN SOUTHAMPTON, VA.

AS FULLY AND VOLUNTARILY MADE TO

THOMAS R. GRAY,

In the prison where he was confined, and acknowledged by him to be such, when read before the Court of Southampton: with the certificate, under seal of the Court convened at Jerusalem, Nov. 5, 1831, for his trial.

ALSO,

AN AUTHENTIC ACCOUNT

OF THE

WHOLE INSURRECTION,

captured and killed. Turner escaped and managed to hide until being discovered on October 30. In less than two weeks, he was tried, hanged, and gruesomely skinned. All told, fifty-five people connected with the rebellion were executed, but the fear and suspicion created by the rebellion spread far. White mobs took to the streets, murdering slaves and free blacks who had nothing to do with the revolt.

Revolt at Sea: The *Amistad*

One of the most famous slave revolts of the nineteenth century took place on the *Amistad*. In August 1839, the U.S. Navy spotted a vessel off the coast of Long Island and thought it was a pirate ship. It was the *Amistad*, commanded by slaves who had mutinied when the ship was traveling between ports in Cuba. The leader of the slaves, Sengbe Pieh, known as Joseph Cinque, thought the ship was sailing back to Africa. The Spanish sailors helping him pilot the ship, however, had secretly turned northward along the U.S. coast.

The U.S. Navy captured the ship and charged the slaves on board with mutiny. Three abolitionists stepped forward as supporters for the slaves and raised funds to provide legal help. Their organization was known as the "*Amistad* Committee."

Initially, at trial in Hartford, Connecticut, Justice Smith Thompson of the U.S. Circuit Court wanted to dismiss the charges of murder and mutiny because the revolt happened on a Spanish vessel. U.S. District Court Justice Andrew

Death of Captain Ferrar, the captain of the *Amistad*

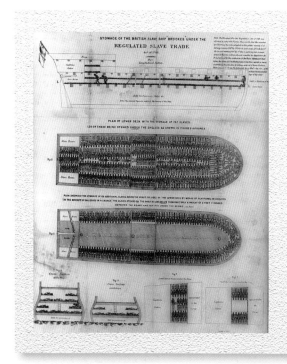

STOWAGE OF THE BRITISH SLAVE SHIP BROOKES UNDER THE
REGULATED SLAVE TRADE

THE AMISTAD

The real *Amistad* was sold, renamed, and disappeared from shipping records after 1844. Today, it is possible to visit a full-scale reconstruction of the *Amistad* and learn more about the fascinating story of the 1839 slave rebellion on the ship. Dubbed the *Freedom Schooner*, the replica ship's home is on the Long Wharf Pier in New Haven, Connecticut (map reference 1), but it makes trips up and down the eastern seaboard, along with occasional jaunts into the Great Lakes. The Freedom Schooner *Amistad* serves as a floating museum and classroom dedicated to improving relations between different races and cultures.

LEFT: The deck plans and cross sections of the British slave ship *Brookes* under the regulated slave trade act of 1788. The illustration shows how slaves were stacked like firewood.

Judson, however, overrode his opinion. The slaves returned to the jail at New Haven and awaited trial.

When interpreters were finally found who could translate the slaves' African languages, the abolitionists discovered fascinating details about the men captured on *Amistad*. They learned that Cinque was a farmer back in Africa and a member of a group called the Mendi. He had a wife and children. Some of the men had been abducted from their homes at night and forced aboard the ship. These details helped build a case for the men and for the abolitionist cause. Learning about the personal lives of people who had been bought and sold as slaves helped undecided white individuals see them as people much like themselves. The *Amistad* case became a rallying point for increasing abolitionist feelings in New England.

Fortunately, things turned out well for Cinque and the thirty-seven other Mendi from the *Amistad*. Judge Judson decided that they were neither slaves nor Spanish subjects and should be granted their wish to return home. For a time, a small Mendi community flourished along with white abolitionists in Farmingham, Connecticut. They stayed for almost a year and then sailed home.

CHAPTER 3
HARRIET TUBMAN'S ESCAPE

When fugitive slaves finally crossed over to freedom in the North, they generally used new names to protect themselves. The noted abolitionist Frederick Douglass is a case in point. Originally Frederick Augustus Washington Bailey, he took on the last name of Douglass—a new name for a new life.

"Harriet" was the name of Tubman's mother, and Tubman may have decided to use it as her new first name after escaping slavery in 1849. No longer "Araminta" or "Minty" from her days of being hired out, she became a new person with her new name.

Harriet probably made her escape sometime in September 1849. Notices in local newspapers shortly afterward mention a reward for a woman, "about 27 years old, by the name of Minty." Harriet made her decision to leave shortly after hearing a rumor that she and other slaves were about to be sold into the Deep South.

Initially, Tubman's brothers, Ben and Henry, were going to go with her. Both of them, however, were terrified of being caught and sold to slavers in the Deep South. Ben was also a young father with a wife and children. If he left then, it was possible he would never see them again. Harriet was very different from her brothers and from most slaves. She was courageous, but, more important, she understood that slavery was a threat to her life. She was willing to fight for her life, and the first step in that fight was escaping.

It is likely that Harriet had been thinking about her escape for some time and had developed a plan for her trip north. Harriet was twenty-seven years old and a smart woman. Slaves often shared rumors about the Underground

Railroad. She undoubtedly combined this information with her knowledge of the surrounding country to figure out the best way to travel the 90 miles (144 km) to freedom. Luckily for Harriet, there were plenty of places to hide along the way north. The marshy landscape of eastern Maryland provided excellent resting spots—hard to see through and tough to track. Also, Quakers and other abolitionists had settled in the region and were generally united against slavery.

Tubman mentions a woman who "gave her a piece of paper with two names upon it and directions on how she might get to the first home." Apparently, Tubman gave the woman a quilt in return for the information—an object that would have slowed her down and probably made her seem more conspicuous anyway.

Of course, the note put Tubman in a tough position. She could not read or write, so she had to rely on the word of a stranger that this piece of paper, handed to the right individual, would help her on her way. It took courage to keep moving northward.

FREDERICK DOUGLASS

Frederick Douglass, one of the United States' most famous abolitionists, was himself an escaped slave. Born in February 1818 in Talbot County, Maryland, Douglass spent his early life only about 30 miles (48 km) from the young Harriet Tubman. Although they would not meet until later in life when both were deeply involved in the abolitionist movement, it is possible that both knew some of the same plantation owners in Maryland.

Douglass came to prominence in 1841, when, three years after his successful escape from slavery, he addressed a meeting of abolitionists led by William Lloyd Garrison. His firsthand experience as a slave, combined with an excellent speaking style, captivated audiences throughout the North. Four years later, his first book, *Narrative of the Life of Frederick Douglass: An American Slave*, catapulted him to fame as a lecturer in the United States and in Great Britain.

Douglass was tireless. He founded a newspaper, the *North Star*, from his home in Rochester, New York. During the war, he helped recruit black soldiers to join the fight against slavery. Following the Civil War, Douglass moved to Washington, D.C., and worked first in the city government, and then as a consul to the governments of Haiti and the Dominican Republic. Visitors can still see the house Douglass lived in from 1877 until his death in 1895. It has been preserved as a national historic site (map reference 8) and is open daily for tours except for New Year's Day, Thanksgiving, and Christmas.

Not too far down the road, at a white-owned farm, Harriet showed the slip of paper to a woman working outside. The woman simply told Tubman to start working, so she began to sweep the front porch. More than likely, this was the farm woman's clever way of throwing off any suspicion. Tubman simply looked like a servant doing her job.

Later the woman's husband came home. He hid Tubman in his wagon, drove her to nearby town, and gave her directions to yet another safe house to stay before heading northward again.

Generally, escaping slaves hid during the day and moved north at night. Trying to blend in during the day was difficult, to say the least, and might have involved staying in abandoned barns, under little-used bridges, or in hollowed-out logs to get a bit of fitful sleep. By dusk, they would be on their way.

The exact route of Harrriet Tubman's escape is still not certain. Her tracks may have crossed Dr. Anthony Thompson's plantation, where Harriet's father Ben was working, and where Harriet herself had worked on and off for the past two years. The nearby town of Poplar Neck, a

Decorative patchwork quilt decorated with a large eight-pointed star

QUILTS AND THE UNDERGROUND RAILROAD

Quilts may have been used as a code language or memory device for freedom seekers hoping to escape on the Underground Railroad. Many slaves could not read or write, but quilt block patterns may have been a way to provide directions. For example, if one slave said to another, "Remember to work on the Bear Paw pattern," it could mean they were to follow a trail through the hills, similar to that taken by a bear. It could also mean that they were supposed to memorize the techniques for making a certain quilt pattern and use that information as a type of map. For example, the mathematics of knots or the shapes of the different blocks might have been translated into directions to follow. Quilts hung outside to "air" may also have been signals—instructing slaves to get ready to move, whether through the woods (like a bear) or for a long journey (as those by wagon or train).

SPRING HILL

Tubman stayed in several safe houses during her rescue trips into the South. Safe houses were found along all of the important routes of the Underground Railroad. Most had special features that their owners used to hide escaping slaves. Many of these unique homes have been preserved and can be visited today, such as Ohio's Spring Hill (map reference 28). This was the home of a prominent Quaker couple, Thomas and Charity Rotch. Involved in the Underground Railroad, they originally housed escaping slaves in the upper story. The house includes additions and secret passages perfectly suited for hiding runaway slaves. A stairway led from a basement to the second story but was hidden from view by anyone stopping by on the first floor. After Thomas and Charity died, in 1823 and 1824, Spring Hill was purchased by the Wales family, who were also abolitionists.

predominantly Quaker settlement, seems like a natural choice as well. Years later, Harriet mentioned that most of the rivers ran in a southern direction in the area where she grew up. Moving upstream alongside one of them could have guided her northward as well.

A photograph from August 1862 showing fugitive African American slaves fording the Rappahannock River

CHAPTER 4
IN THE NORTH

Crossing into Delaware—officially a free state—provided some relief for an escaping slave like Harriet, but just making it across the Mason-Dixon line did not guarantee safety. Though a free state, Delaware, as well as as many Northern states, still harbored plenty of proslavery sentiment.

After getting close to Wilmington, Delaware, Harriet was only miles away from Pennsylvania—a more hospitable place for a slave on the run than Delaware, which was known for roving bands of slave catchers and bounty hunters. Crossing the Delaware state line into Pennsylvania, Tubman said she had to "look at my hands to see if I was the same person. . . . I felt like I was in heaven."

In Pennsylvania, Harriet might have met up with two important "stationmasters" of the Underground Railroad—Isaac and Dinah Mendenhall. Like their real railroad counterparts, Underground Railroad stationmasters were in charge of important stopping places along the escape routes. The Mendenhall's home was a beautiful brick house with a square concealed room built between a large fireplace and the carriage house. The only way into the concealed room was through a loft. Although the exact number of freedom seekers aided by the Mendenhalls is not known, it is estimated in the hundreds. Their home was one of the first stops in Pennsylvania for anyone coming off the "Wilmington Line" of the Underground Railroad. "Passengers" were sent to the house by abolitionist Thomas Garrett of Wilmington, who told them, "keep traveling on and on until you see a stone gate post—then turn in." The house is still there today.

On a good night, an escaped slave might be able to cover about 10 miles (16 km)—especially with help from conductors

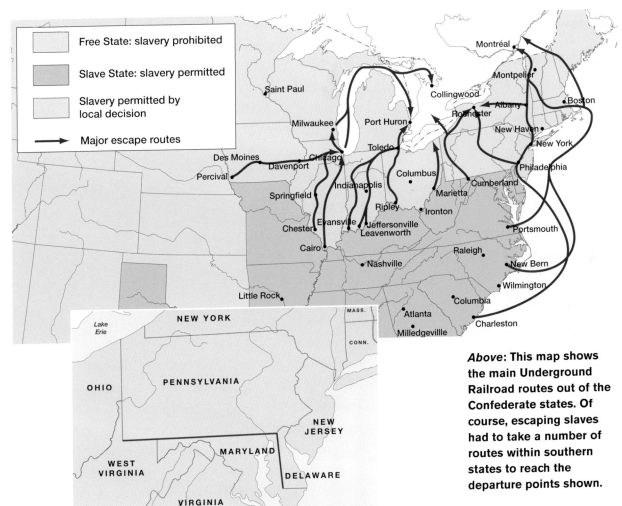

Above: This map shows the main Underground Railroad routes out of the Confederate states. Of course, escaping slaves had to take a number of routes within southern states to reach the departure points shown.

Left: Map showing the Mason-Dixon Line—usually seen as the dividing line between the North and South. The line was surveyed by colonial surveyors Charles Mason and Jeremiah Dixon in the 1700s to settle a boundary dispute; their names have stuck.

from the Underground Railroad. By the time Tubman arrived in Philadelphia, she had traveled more than 100 miles (160 km)—mostly on foot. How long did it take? No one knows for certain—anywhere from ten days to three weeks.

Philadelphia was a good place to blend into a crowd. The city already had a sizeable free black population. Even by the 1830s, one-twelfth of the population was black. The abolitionist society in Philadelphia was one of the nation's oldest. In fact, Benjamin Franklin founded the Pennsylvania Society for the Promotion of Abolition of Slavery.

Although there is not much information about the work Harriet did after settling down in Philadelphia, she could have easily found employment as kitchen help or as a nurse. As much of an improvement as Philadelphia was over life in slavery, it still had its drawbacks. Like any border state, slave catchers still made the rounds—abducting African Americans,

BETHEL AFRICAN METHODIST EPISCOPAL CHURCH

In nineteenth-century Pennsylvania, African-American churches thrived, including the African Methodist Episcopal (AME) Church, which played a large part in Harriet's spiritual growth. One of these churches, the Bethel AME Church, is still open to the public in Reading, Pennsylvania (map reference 2). Jacob Ross (not related to Tubman's father), one of the founding members, was himself an escaped slave. The congregation was active in support of the Underground Railroad.

often children, to sell as slaves in the South. Also, not all white residents in Philadelphia were opposed to slavery. Tension grew between proslavery whites and the increasingly outspoken abolitionists. As a result, mobs of angry white gangs took out their frustrations on black neighborhoods. There were five different antiblack riots in Philadelphia between 1837 and 1842. Poor Irish immigrants, who competed with the free blacks for jobs, initiated most of the violence.

Meeting William Still

By the time Harriet Tubman met William Still in Philadelphia, he was already well known. His father, Levin Still, was a slave who had purchased his own freedom. His mother, Charity, had been a runaway slave.

William Still was born in New Jersey in 1821 and moved to Philadelphia when he was twenty-three years old. Three years later, in 1847, he married and became active in the Philadelphia Society for the Abolition of Slavery.

By 1851, he had begun keeping careful records of all of the escaping slaves moving through society member's "stations," including the famous Johnson House. He interviewed freedom seekers and recorded their circumstances in enough detail to present an excellent account of the conditions of slaves and stories of their escape during the period. Still even included press clippings, slave notices, and other stories that related to the various escapees, providing even more documentation. Because this information would have been dangerous if it fell into the wrong hands, Still hid his notes in the attic of a local seminary and in a nearby graveyard. Shortly after the Civil War, in 1867, he gathered these notes together to compile his own book of slave narratives.

The Escape of Henry Brown

Probably the most famous slave Still had the opportunity to meet was Henry "Box" Brown. He worked in a tobacco factory, he married, had children, and rented a home. Nonetheless, he and his family were still slaves, and his wife had a different owner. In 1849, Henry's wife and children were sold. That was enough for him. Saddened over the loss of his family, he was determined to escape.

THE JOHNSON HOUSE

Five generations of the Johnson family occupied this Philadelphia house starting in 1768. The Johnsons were Quakers and abolitionists; they operated their home as a station on the Underground Railroad. They were known to collaborate with Tubman and Still in their efforts to help fugitive slaves. Today the home is a National Historic Landmark and a museum dedicated to the Underground Railroad (map reference 19).

The Johnson House, built in 1768, stands in the Germantown district of Philadelphia, Pennsylvania.

A white abolitionist in Richmond, Virginia, Samuel Smith, and a free black friend, James Caesar Anthony Smith, helped Brown with his plan. They built a wooden box, big enough to fit Henry, drilled air holes in it, painted "This Side Up" on the outside, and threw in a small canteen or "bladder" of water and some biscuits for the trip. Brown then had himself shipped to Philadelphia. As he told it, most porters and baggage handlers ignored the "This Side Up" painted on the box, so he spent part of the trip upside down. He made it safely to Philadelphia, and William Still was there when the box lid was removed. Brown stood up, reached out his hand, and exclaimed, "How do you do, gentlemen?"

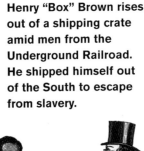

Henry "Box" Brown rises out of a shipping crate amid men from the Underground Railroad. He shipped himself out of the South to escape from slavery.

Because William Still was such a major force behind the organized Underground Railroad in Philadelphia, it is likely that he was one of the first people Harriet encountered on her arrival. Still probably was the person who taught Harriet how the Underground Railroad worked and gave her the knowledge— and encouragement— that she needed to conduct her many rescue trips into the South.

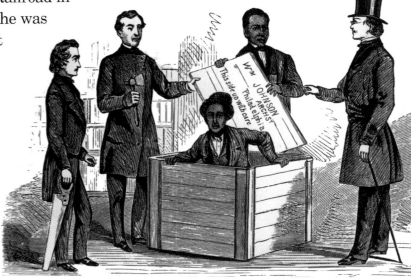

CHAPTER 5
THE FUGITIVE SLAVE ACT

Not long after Harriet reached Philadelphia, Congress passed the Fugitive Slave Act. The legislation emerged as part of the Compromise of 1850, which allowed California into the Union as a free state, a state that did not allow slavery. Congress considered it a way to "even the balance" of having another free state in the country.

Abolitionists called the Fugitive Slave Act, the "Man-Stealing Law" or the "Bloodhound Law." The law considered any aid to escaping slaves—including offering them food, shelter, or clothing—a federal crime. Violating the law meant a possible $1,000 fine and six months in prison. Suspected slaves were not offered the usual protection provided to free citizens—black or white—by the Constitution. For example, they could not request a jury trial or testify on their own behalf.

The law used a bounty system to encourage slave catchers. They were paid $10 for every escaped black slave they brought back but only $5 for a black man or woman was discovered to be free—creating many cases of entire free black families being apprehended as "runaway slaves."

The new law was so unpopular in the North that President Millard Fillmore considered sending troops to Boston to force inhabitants to obey. Because of the turmoil caused by the new law, Harriet Tubman knew she had to keep moving north and that Canada was really the only option. As much as it must have pained her to be so far from her family, her drive never to be a slave again pushed her onward.

Rescuing Her Family

Harriet had not been in Philadelphia for very long when she heard news from her old home in Dorchester County—and it was not good. The Brodess plantation was short on cash, and

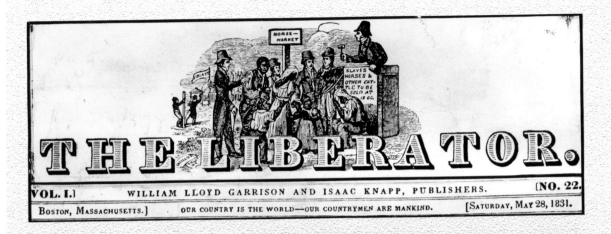

THE LIBERATOR.

VOL. I.]   WILLIAM LLOYD GARRISON AND ISAAC KNAPP, PUBLISHERS.   [NO. 22.

BOSTON, MASSACHUSETTS.]   OUR COUNTRY IS THE WORLD—OUR COUNTRYMEN ARE MANKIND.   [SATURDAY, MAY 28, 1831.

WILLIAM LLOYD GARRISON

William Lloyd Garrison was one of America's best-known abolitionists, and he was a friend of Harriet Tubman. The two met during one of Harriet's many trips to Boston, a city in which she gave talks about her experiences on the Underground Railroad. Garrison was considered so dangerous to slave-holding states that in 1831 the state of Georgia offered a reward for his arrest. Born in 1805 in Newburyport, Massachusetts, Garrison became an apprentice to a newspaper editor when he was only thirteen years old. Shortly after his apprenticeship ended, he became co-owner of a newspaper, the *Free Press*. It folded after only six months, but during that time, Garrison became known as a staunch abolitionist. After working as an editor in Boston, then Baltimore, Garrison returned to Boston and launched the *Liberator*, an anti-slavery newspaper.

Garrison was a popular and fiery lecturer, delivering impassioned pleas to end slavery to large audiences. He was also controversial. Though committed to nonviolent resistance, some of his methods of protest were unorthodox; at an antislavery rally on July 4, 1854, he burned a copy of the United States Constitution, delighting the crowd of three thousand cheering supporters.

When the Civil War ended and emancipation was finally a reality, Garrison published his final issue of the *Liberator* on December 29, 1865. He was far from being done protesting, however, and he devoted the years until his death in 1879 to other reform movements, including temperance (anti-alcohol) and women's suffrage (the right to vote).

Garrison's Boston home is privately owned and not open to the public, but it is part of the Black Heritage Trail and the Boston African-American National Historic Site. Ranger-guided tours explore fourteen sites related to Boston's nineteenth-century free black community.

Above: Letterhead of the William Lloyd Garrison campaigning paper the *Liberator* published in Boston, Massachusetts, and dated May 28, 1831.
Right: William Lloyd Garrison.

even though Harriet was gone, there were still "too many slaves" and too much debt that remained to be settled. Word had filtered to Tubman that her niece Kessiah (known mostly

A typical slave pen at Alexandria, Virginia. The barred gate opens onto a courtyard and the doors to six pens.

by her nickname, "Kizzy") was going to be auctioned off at the Dorchester County Courthouse in Cambridge, Massachusetts.

Tubman quickly made her way down to Baltimore, and she stayed with friends. The city's waterfront was an easy place to stay because many of Tubman's friends, free black men and women, originally from Dorchester, lived and worked there. In Baltimore, Harriet planned an escape for Kessiah and her two children with the help of Kessiah's husband, John Browley, a freeman.

The day of the auction came, and the usual crowd of buyers and spectators formed a crowd in front of the courthouse. The auction for Kessiah and her children went ahead without interruption, and her buyer and John Brodess, acting for the plantation, settled the sale. The auctioneer stepped out briefly while Kessiah and her children were taken from the courthouse steps.

The auctioneer returned shortly afterward, but no one came up to pay for the sale. He was just about ready to start the auction for Kessiah all over again when he realized that neither she nor her children were anywhere in sight. Amazingly, no one realized at the time that the "buyer" was, in fact, Kessiah's husband! (It would not have been unusual for a black man to buy slaves. In fact, many free blacks owned black slaves.) John Browley hid his wife and children in a safe house only five minutes from the auction and later loaded them in a small boat and sailed up the Chesapeake Bay to Baltimore. Harriet met the family there and escorted them to Philadelphia.

Harriet's second rescue trip took place only a few months later. On this mission, she retrieved one of her brothers (there is some debate as to which one, Moses—so skillfully hidden by her mother years before—or James) and two other men. Apparently, they had already run away when Harriet found them. She helped them safely reach the home of Thomas Garret, the most famous stationmaster on the Underground Railroad.

During her third journey, in December 1851, Harriet tried to convince her husband, John Tubman, to return north with her. Sadly, Harriet learned that in her absence, he had remarried and would not leave his new wife. In spite of this disappointment, she still managed to bring eleven slaves, including her brother, William Henry, and his wife, Catherine, out of Dorchester. This was her largest operation yet.

Tubman's long road north to New York, and then to Canada, may have included a

Below left: Wilson Chinn, a branded slave from Louisiana, photographed in about 1863. Beside him are some instruments of torture used to punish slaves.

Below right: An abolitionist poster from Massachusetts, dated 1850, condemns the Fugitive Slave Law and the Massachusetts politicians who voted for it.

stop at the home of the famous abolitionist, Frederick Douglass. In one of his later writings, Douglass mentions the large group and says, "I had difficulty providing so many with food and shelter, but . . . they were content with very plain food and a strip of carpet on the floor for a bed, or a place on the straw in the barn loft." At the end of their stay, Douglass helped Tubman and her company board a train bound for the border and the suspension bridge that led to St. Catherines, Ontario, Canada, and freedom.

Because it was December when they arrived, and because she lacked warm clothes, Tubman stayed in St. Catherines for several months, working to build up supplies and money for another journey. Local groups helped out, and many of the escaped slaves earned money chopping firewood or hiring out as domestic help as Tubman did. By spring, she had made enough money to go back to Philadelphia. Once there, she worked all summer as a cook and then returned to Dorchester again, this time leading out a group of nine slaves.

Harriet Tubman—on the extreme left holding a pan—photographed with a group of slaves she helped escape

CHAPTER 6
BECOMING "MOSES"

Over the next few years, Philadelphia and St. Catherines both served as part-time homes for Tubman. Philadelphia, with its well-organized abolitionist and Underground Railroad communities, was an excellent base of operations for her rescues. St. Catherines, safely across the Canadian border, was the best possible place for escaping slaves to call home; in Canada, no Fugitive Slave Act could touch them.

During the years in Philadelphia, Tubman became known by another name: Moses. The new code name suited Harriet well. She was, after all, a deeply religious person leading people to freedom. At least once and sometimes twice every year, Tubman sneaked back into her home territory alone. She did not want to endanger the lives of fugitive slaves who already had earned their freedom.

In 1857, Harriet was able to rescue her parents—and probably just in time. Although her father was a freeman, he had recently come under suspicion of harboring fugitive slaves. He had let eight freedom seekers spend the night in his cabin a few months before. They may have been, in fact, the famous "Dover Eight." This group of runaway slaves had been captured and jailed in Dover, Delaware. They escaped the jail, and their getaway set off a storm of publicity in Maryland and Delaware. This was a delicate

135,000 SETS, 270,000 VOLUMES SOLD.

UNCLE TOM'S CABIN

FOR SALE HERE.

AN EDITION FOR THE MILLION, COMPLETE IN 1 Vol. PRICE 37 1-2 CENTS.
"   "   IN GERMAN, IN 1 Vol. PRICE 50 CENTS.
"   "   IN 2 Vols. CLOTH, 6 PLATES, PRICE $1.50.
SUPERB ILLUSTRATED EDITION, IN 1 Vol, WITH 153 ENGRAVINGS,
PRICES FROM $2.50 TO $5.00.

The Greatest Book of the Age.

A poster advertising Harriet Beecher Stowe's best-selling antislavery novel, *Uncle Tom's Cabin*, written in 1852

Right: Title page from
the first edition of *Uncle
Tom's Cabin* by Harriet
Beecher Stowe

UNCLE TOM'S CABIN;

OR,

LIFE AMONG THE LOWLY.

BY

HARRIET BEECHER STOWE.

VOL. I.

BOSTON:
JOHN P. JEWETT & COMPANY.
CLEVELAND, OHIO:
JEWETT, PROCTOR & WORTHINGTON.
1852.

FIRST EDITION, IN THE EXCESSIVELY RARE
RED CLOTH PRESENTATION BINDING

**Harriet Beecher Stowe
(1811-1896), American
novelist and humanitarian,
became internationally
renowned for her book
Uncle Tom's Cabin.**

time for Harriet to rescue her parents.

Unlike many of Harriet's other journeys, the one to rescue her parents took place in the spring. Perhaps because Harriet's parents were so old, she did not want them to suffer any more hardships than they had to. A trip to Canada along the Underground Railroad was not easy any time of year.

Harriet's father made a rough horse cart for him and Harriet's mother to travel on. Harriet led her parents to Wilmington, Delaware, using her Underground Railroad contacts, and then on to Philadelphia, where they met up with William Still.

Tubman returned South again that summer, planning to find her sister Rachel and her children. Once there, Harriet discovered that Rachel had been hired out to another farm and was separated from her children; it was impossible to gather together and rescue the family at that time. Even though no one came back with Harriet on that trip, she helped organize a group of thirty-nine slaves who escaped later that year.

Common Rescue Techniques

It is amazing to consider that one woman—an escaped slave—could travel alone into the South so many times and rescue so many people. To be successful, Harriet Tubman developed a variety of techniques that she used to arrange escapes, to keep escaping slaves safe and calm, and to travel unnoticed in slave country.

Harriet Tubman was deeply religious and often sang hymns and spirituals along the way to calm the worried

Above: Novelist Harriet Beecher Stowe and her husband, Rev. Calvin Ellis Stowe (1802–1886), with three friends on the porch of their Florida residence in about 1881.

HARRIET BEECHER STOWE

Harriet Beecher Stowe wrote the widely read book *Uncle Tom's Cabin*, which exposed the cruel world of Southern slavery and fueled the abolitionist movement. Originally from Litchfield, Connecticut, Stowe moved with her family to Ohio in 1832. Her firsthand experiences witnessing slavery in nearby Kentucky and interviews with fugitive slaves, including Josiah Henson (who escaped to Canada via the Underground Railroad), provided the basis for her book. In 1850, she moved to Maine, where her husband had accepted a teaching position. It was there that she wrote her famous book; it was published in 1852. Two of the homes that Stowe lived in during her life—in Cincinnati, Ohio (map reference 11), and in Brunswick, Maine—have been preserved as museums dedicated to her life.

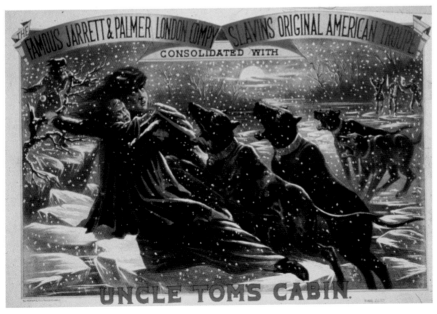

Left: Dating from about 1850, a poster for a theater production of *Uncle Tom's Cabin*

This photograph is entitled "Group of contraband at Follers House, Cumberland Landing, Va., May, 1862." *Contraband* means "illegal goods." Since slaves were regarded as the property of their owner and escape was illegal, these people are considered "illegal goods," or "contraband."

minds of the escaping slaves she guided. She was tough, however, and realistic, too. She carried a pistol as protection against slave catchers and those in her party who threatened to turn back.

There are no records that Tubman actually used the pistol on anyone thinking of retreat, but one slave, Henry Carrol, did not stop long to find out. At one point during his escape, guided by Tubman, he wanted to rest. Slave catchers were closing in and Tubman's response was to the point. "Go on or die," she told him. Carrol moved right along.

Harriet also timed her rescues well, waiting until Saturday night to depart because no newspapers—meaning no missing slave notices—were printed on Sunday. It gave escaping slaves a day's head start without publicity. Winter was a favorite season for escapes, difficult as the weather was, because the nights were longer.

Harriet arranged meeting places with escaping slaves up to 10 miles (16 km) away from the plantations, and she was careful never to be seen on the plantations. At least in one instance, she chose a cemetery for a meeting place—one of the few public spaces African Americans could meet without arousing suspicion.

Tubman also used some of the money she raised to pay sympathetic whites and free blacks to tear down the notices advertising escaped slaves to help cover their tracks. On occasion, she would take a train into the South because it seemed less suspicious to be traveling so openly, especially heading into slave territory. An admiring abolitionist once remarked, "Fugitives in Moses' care were never captured."

Harriet could not read, but she carried a book with her anyway. It came in handy as part of her disguise when operating south of the Mason-Dixon line. Once she overheard two white men talking about a description of her on a wanted poster. One of them mentioned that it said she could not read. Harriet took out a book before they passed by and seemed completely engrossed in the story. On another occasion, she spotted a former master (one she had been hired out to years before) in the same train car. She simply picked up the newspaper and "read" it calmly.

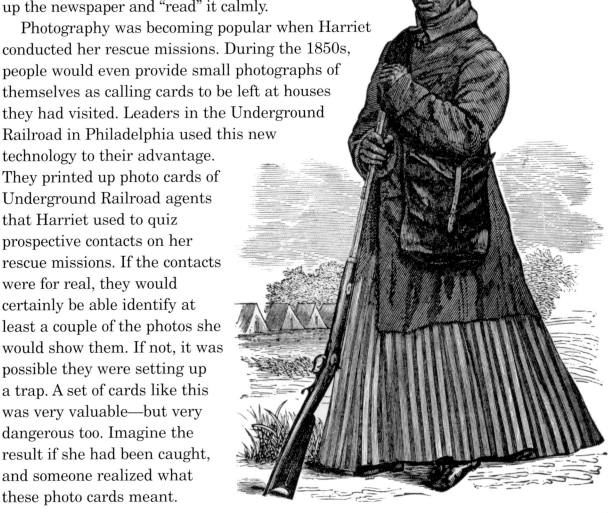

An undated woodcut of Harriet Tubman

Photography was becoming popular when Harriet conducted her rescue missions. During the 1850s, people would even provide small photographs of themselves as calling cards to be left at houses they had visited. Leaders in the Underground Railroad in Philadelphia used this new technology to their advantage. They printed up photo cards of Underground Railroad agents that Harriet used to quiz prospective contacts on her rescue missions. If the contacts were for real, they would certainly be able identify at least a couple of the photos she would show them. If not, it was possible they were setting up a trap. A set of cards like this was very valuable—but very dangerous too. Imagine the result if she had been caught, and someone realized what these photo cards meant.

CHAPTER 7
KEEPING SAFE ON THE JOURNEY

Like any secret enterprise, the Underground Railroad had a code all its own. The very name "Underground Railroad" is a case in point. Although the term came to be understood by a wide audience (proslavery and abolitionist alike), the name began as a way to disguise its actual purpose—freeing slaves. Anyone casually overhearing railroad-related terms like *station* or *conductor* might just ignore the conversation, figuring it had to do with a timetable or a depot somewhere. Knocking on the doors of these safe houses and depots usually required memorizing a secret knock—one that let people inside know that guests were waiting outside who could not linger there for long.

In some sections of the Underground Railroad, making the sound of an owl was a popular call to check for other conductors ahead. When members of the Underground Railroad wrote letters to each other, they sometimes referred to their passengers as *cargo* or *bales*.

Conventional codes like these weren't the only way to send signals on the Underground Railroad. Harriet Tubman sometimes used songs to deliver messages to her passengers. She would change the tempo of songs—often making them slow or sad to warn of danger ahead. Then she would change them back to something upbeat to let people know that everything was "all clear."

Songs also helped remind people of the direction to freedom. One famous song included the saying, "Follow the drinking gourd." The *drinking gourd* was a code word for the Big Dipper constellation, shaped like a ladle and pointing to the North Star. It provided a ready compass on clear nights on the road.

The Drinking Gourd song sung by escaping slaves was a code that helped the travelers follow the road north to freedom. The "drinking gourd" refers to the Big Dipper constellation and its built-in compass; it is believed that the "big river" named in the song is the Tennessee River and the "little river" is the Ohio.

The riverbank will make a very good road
The dead trees show you the way
Left foot, peg foot, traveling on
Follow the drinking gourd

Chorus:
Follow the drinking gourd
Follow the drinking gourd
For the old man is a-waiting to take you to freedom
If you follow the drinking gourd

The river ends between two hills
Follow the drinking gourd
There's another river on the other side
Follow the drinking gourd
Chorus

Where the great big river meets the little river
Follow the drinking gourd
The old man is a-waiting to take you to freedom
If you follow the drinking gourd
Chorus

On a clear night, the Big Dipper (shown here) would help guide the way to safety for fugitive slaves.

Safe Houses and Depots

Running a depot or a safe house was a tricky operation. Abolitionists, black and white, took a huge risk by hiding from authorities the fact that they provided a haven for escaping slaves. There were safe houses, conductors, and depots scattered throughout the states, especially east of the Mississippi. The following are three of the most famous safe houses, and all are preserved as historic sites.

The Levi Coffin House (map reference 22)

The Levi Coffin House, a National Historic Landmark, is located in Fountain City, Indiana. Levi Coffin was a Quaker and originally from North Carolina. Levi and his

Above: In 1810, the Reverend Alexander Dobbin created sliding shelves to conceal a crawl space at his Gettysburg, Pennsylvania, home to hide several slaves.

Below: Among the 2,000 slaves Levi Coffin assisted, William Bush, a settler of Newport, reached Levi's house wearing wooden shoes. William became a conductor for other runaway slaves.

wife, Catherine, were committed abolitionists who hid escaped slaves in their basement. They usually had a wagon and horses hitched up and ready to go on a moment's notice. Years after the Civil War, Coffin said, "Frequently wagon loads of passengers from different lines would meet at our house. . . . The companies varied in number, from two or three fugitives to seventeen."

Coffin later mentioned that the route to freedom was dangerous and tough. Even using a horse-drawn wagon, the "journeys had to be made at night, often through deep mud and bad roads, and along byways that were seldom traveled." Often slave catchers would already be on the lookout—sometimes even waiting ahead of Coffin and his passengers.

It is estimated that the Coffins helped 2,000 to 3,000 slaves escape to freedom. Coffin was dubbed the "president" of the Underground Railroad for his many abolitionist activities, including operating a store in Cincinnati that dealt only in "free labor" goods (merchandise not made by slaves or slave-associated industries). He also organized an association that contributed money and clothing to newly free men, women, and children.

John Rankin House (map reference 18)

The John Rankin House in Ripley, Ohio, is a National Historic Landmark. Rankin was a Presbyterian minister

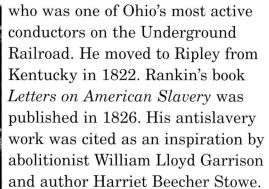

who was one of Ohio's most active conductors on the Underground Railroad. He moved to Ripley from Kentucky in 1822. Rankin's book *Letters on American Slavery* was published in 1826. His antislavery work was cited as an inspiration by abolitionist William Lloyd Garrison and author Harriet Beecher Stowe.

Providing a literal guiding light for slaves on the southern side of the Ohio River, Rankin made sure to have a lantern set out at night for all to see.

Rankin's entire family (he and his wife had thirteen children) helped slaves escape northward for decades, beginning in the 1820s and continuing right through the close of the Civil War. Most of the two thousand escaping slaves that passed through Ripley stayed with the Rankins; they proudly boasted that they never lost a passenger.

Presbyterian minister John Rankin was one of the organizers of the Underground Railroad.

The Milton House (map reference 23)

Milton House is a three-story structure built with a unique, stuccolike appearance and the words "Milton House" painted on the sides. A residence and an inn in southern Wisconsin, it was built by Joseph Goodrich, originally from Massachusetts. Goodrich, with a group of other Seventh-Day Adventists, built a log cabin in the area in 1838. He and his family moved to Milton, Wisconsin, permanently the next year and stayed in the cabin while building the first Milton House. By 1845, the structure that stands today was built. The cabin remained as an outbuilding on the property.

Escaping slaves would enter the old log cabin about 40 feet (12 meters) from the main house and then head through a trap door and tunnel to the basement of the Milton House for food and shelter. It seems that the tunnel was built specifically for this purpose when the inn was being completed. Originally much smaller, it was expanded in the 1950s for tours. Today the Milton House is a National Historic Landmark that is open for tours.

In the Wisconsin wilderness in 1844, five years after founding the town of Milton, Joseph Goodrich built a hexagonal inn and hand dug a tunnel from the inn's basement to a root cellar 40 feet (12 m) away to hide slaves.

CHAPTER 8
MEETING JOHN BROWN

St. Catherines, Ontario, had become a home for many former slaves and for much of Harriet Tubman's family. By 1858, Tubman was already well known to many famous abolitionists, including Frederick Douglass, William Lloyd Garrison, and John Brown.

John Brown met with Harriet Tubman in St. Catherines while trying to build support for his plan to raid the federal arsenal at Harper's Ferry, Virginia. Prior to the meeting, Tubman believed she'd had a vision of John Brown—a recurring dream she couldn't interpret until she met Brown face to face.

Tubman was reportedly impressed with Brown, and he with her. It seemed natural—they were both people of action. Although their initial meeting in Canada was brief, a short time later they met again in Boston. Harriet was raising funds for the community of former slaves in Canada, and Brown was raising funds and trying to enlist more troops for his plans. Apparently, they met often, and Brown took to referring to Harriet as "General Tubman"; he considered her "a better officer than most." They pored over plans like military leaders launching an invasion; Tubman even suggested that the Fourth of July was the best time to attack Harper's Ferry. Her knowledge of terrain and her contacts with safe houses along the Underground Railroad were probably very helpful to John Brown. In fact, there is evidence that Harriet Tubman may have been a big part of Brown's original plans for the attack. It seems that he hoped for her participation, at least by doing some advance scouting work.

It is not certain why Harriet declined to join Brown on his raid. It's possible she was ill or that she was already in

Maryland preparing for a rescue trip. Given her bravery and the daring rescues during the previous nine years, it was unlikely she was afraid of the consequences. Maybe, like Frederick Douglass, she simply sensed that the Harper's Ferry raid would not go well. Either way, after the raid, she moved quickly to return to safety in Canada.

Harriet Tubman's rescue missions ended just before the start of the Civil War. The number of slaves she helped to freedom varies—estimates range from eighty to more than three hundred, depending on the accounts. No matter what the final count, the incredible bravery Tubman showed in returning thirteen times (or nineteen times, by some

The *Last Moments of John Brown*. Etching by Thomas Hovenden, 1885.

Government forces attack John Brown and his men in the armory.

counts) to lead others to freedom (including her parents)—all while evading possible capture and execution—is amazing.

Harriet Tubman's last rescue trip came in November 1860. She returned to Dorchester County to bring back her sister, Rachel, and Rachel's two children, not realizing that Rachel had died shortly before the trip. Rachel's children could not be retrieved, but in order that some good come of the trip, Harriet helped a family of five, including a baby, move north to freedom.

This last trip was a tough one. The weather was terrible, with freezing rain and sleet. At one point, the baby had to be drugged with opium to keep it calm. Otherwise, patrols looking for runaway slaves could find them by its crying. Worse yet, the escape hadn't been carefully planned, so there were no provisions—no dry clothes or extra food.

Nonetheless, under Tubman's guidance the family made it to freedom. Harriet was deeply disturbed, however, by the new knowledge of her sister's death. Combined with the bad weather's effect on her health, she may have known it would be her final journey as a conductor for the Underground Railroad.

JOHN BROWN

John Brown is one of the most controversial figures in the antislavery movement. Often compared to an Old Testament biblical prophet, his methods might be considered terrorist today.

Brown was born in Torrington, Connecticut, on May 9, 1800. He received little formal schooling, but he read the Bible daily, which was normal for anyone growing up in a religious family at the time. His parents were ardently antislavery, and Brown never forgot the first time he met a slave, whom he described as "badly clothed, poorly fed, and beaten with iron shovels or anything that came first to hand."

In 1848, Brown met Frederick Douglass. By then Douglass was famous as an author and lecturer, and he invited Brown to his home in Massachusetts. Douglass was used to meeting with enthusiastic white abolitionists who always sounded as if they wanted to help but didn't necessarily follow through. Douglass noticed "the fire in Brown's eyes," but probably had no idea how far Brown would go.

By 1855, John Brown and five of his sons had moved to Kansas and formed an armed militia called the "Liberty Guards" in an attempt to keep slaveholders from moving into the territory. After proslavery forces attacked the town of Lawrence, Kansas, Brown and his sons ruthlessly killed proslavery settlers, none of whom had been involved in the raid.

By 1859, Brown formulated an idea—create a republic of freed slaves somewhere in the Appalachian Mountains. He met with Frederick Douglass again to enlist his help. Douglass backed away from the plan—possibly knowing it would be a disaster.

Inspired by the story of Harriet Tubman and the example of Frederick Douglass, Brown launched a raid on a federal arsenal at Harper's Ferry, Virginia (now West Virginia), on October 10, 1859. Brown's goal was to get other slaves and freed blacks to join his fight, but his attack on Harper's Ferry turned out for the worse. His twenty-two men, white and black, crept into town, took over the arsenal and rifle works, and also rounded up sixty local citizens to hold as hostages. At this point, Brown's plan faltered. His hoped-for slave revolt never developed, and the local militia attacked the arsenal, trying to free the hostages. Word of the attack quickly reached Washington, D.C., and Colonel Robert E. Lee was sent to lead an army raid against Brown's men at the arsenal; they were quickly overwhelmed and captured. Less than two months later, on December 2, 1859, Brown was executed. His last words were haunting: "I, John Brown, am now quite certain that the crimes of this guilty land will never be purged away but with blood."

Visitors can still see the John Brown cabin in Osawatomie (map reference 15), Kansas, Harpers Ferry National Historic Park in West Virginia (map reference 9), and the John Brown home and graves in Lake Placid, New York (map reference 16).

CHAPTER 9

HARRIET TUBMAN AND THE CIVIL WAR

After decades of tension between slave states in the South and free states in the North, the Civil War began in April 1861 when the Confederates (the army of the South) shelled Fort Sumter, South Carolina. Eight months later, the governor of Massachusetts, John Andrew, wanted Harriet Tubman to assist the Union war effort. He arranged for her to travel south to Union-occupied territory in South Carolina to work first as a nurse and teacher—though Harriet gained much greater fame later when she became a scout and a spy for the Union army.

Because Harriet knew the Southern terrain and had so much experience traveling in secrecy, she was a natural choice as a scout, gathering intelligence for the army. She also could help the Union army leadership work with the streams of "contrabands"—slaves that had crossed over to Northern lines seeking freedom and a chance to fight the Confederates.

Months passed with Harriet distributing clothes and supplies to the large refugee slave populations that were forming in the territory occupied by the Union army. She worked as a nurse in the camps near Port Royal, South Carolina, a swampy region, perfect for mosquitoes and the diseases they carried. She led a band of scouts to patrol the marshes there, which probably reminded her of those in Dorchester County.

She met General David Hunter in South Carolina. He was an abolitionist who wanted to recruit black soldiers. Although many Africans Americans from Northern cities had volunteered to fight in the Union army since the beginning of the war, they had been

Although the reasons for the Civil War were many, in a sense Fort Sumter is where it all started. For months after the election of President Lincoln, Southern states voiced their intention to leave the republic. By December 20, 1860, South Carolinian delegates had drawn up a declaration to secede, and by March, six more states followed South Carolina's lead. Together they formed the Confederate States of America.

At first, Lincoln didn't think secession would last. Most white Southerners didn't own slaves, and that alone was enough for him to think the crisis would blow over. He underestimated the desire of secessionists to split from the Union.

Fort Sumter, a Union base commanded by Major Robert Anderson, had been cut off from supplies since Christmas. In the first week of April 1861, Lincoln informed the governor of South Carolina that he intended to resupply Anderson's men.

Shortly after midnight on April 12, a delegation from South Carolina rowed out to Fort Sumter and informed Anderson that he had until 4:00 A.M. to surrender the fort. After that, they would open fire. Major Anderson refused.

At 4:30 a.m. the attack came as promised. General Pierre Gustave Toutant Beauregard commanded the artillery for the Confederate side. More than three thousand shells were fired on the fort from Confederate gunners, and the fight drew spectators who watched the battle from the rooftops of Charleston. Amazingly, the only fatality during the entire thirty-four-hour battle was a horse. Anderson and his men were allowed to sail north after calling a truce.

After the bombardment of Fort Sumter, North Carolina, Virginia, Tennessee, and Arkansas joined the new Confederate States of America, headed by President Jefferson Davis.

You can still visit the Fort Sumter National Monument, located in the Charleston harbor (map reference 7). The site is open daily (closed for Christmas and New Year's Day). There is a visitor's center on the mainland, and a park ferry and private tour boat operators provide transportation to the island on which the fort is located.

Above: **Bombardment of Fort Sumter, Charleston Harbor, April 12–13, 1861.**
Right: **The president of the South, Jefferson Davis.**

turned down as soldiers. Hunter, however, organized a group of former slaves in 1862 from an area in South Carolina that the Union occupied. He trained them as the first South Carolina Volunteers. On January 1, 1863, when the Emancipation Proclamation was officially to go into effect, Hunter's soldiers were ready.

The first South Carolina Volunteers were put under the command of General Thomas Wentworth Higginson. Another group of black soldiers became the Second South Carolina volunteers, led by James Montgomery, an old friend of John Brown's from his days in Kansas. Soon both groups of South Carolina Volunteers were battle-tested in an attack on Jacksonville, Florida. Although the resistance was

Photograph of Abraham Lincoln

The Emancipation Proclamation

EMANCIPATION PROCLAMATION

On September 22, 1862, following the Northern victory at the battle of Antietam, President Abraham Lincoln announced the Emancipation Proclamation. Although Lincoln's proclamation had no legal power in the ten rebelling states, it had a tremendous effect on the course of the Civil War because it focused the war more clearly on freeing the slaves. In the eyes of many abolitionists, Lincoln finally was beginning to get the point.

Early in the war, Lincoln was afraid that the border states would lose sympathy with the Union cause if the North accepted black soldiers into the army. He did not wish to push these states into the Confederacy, so African Americans were turned down when they volunteered to fight. As the war progressed, sentiment changed, and after the delivery of the Emancipation Proclamation, thousands of Northern blacks rallied to the cause and were accepted as soldiers. After all, these were men (and a few women, including Harriet Tubman) who had the strongest reasons to fight.

The actual Emancipation Proclamation and other important documents from United States history are on display at the National Archives in Washington, D.C. (map reference 25). The document is also available online at the National Archives Web site.

Newly freed slave family reading the Emancipation Proclamation

lighter than expected, it gave the men confidence and experience for an upcoming raid that Harriet Tubman would help lead.

Harriet had already explored much of the Port Royal area. In the weeks before June 1863, she and her scouts checked the rivers and waterways for mines, the local terrain for Confederate troop positions, and warehouses for supplies of food and weapons. Her hard work developing a network of spies was paying off.

On the first day of June, she was in one of several Union gunboats slowly making its way into the South Carolina interior along the region's narrow waterways. Before long, the boats landed at the plantations Tubman knew contained Confederate supplies.

Black troops swarmed over the countryside, handily taking out Confederate guards and setting fire to plantations, barns, and farm equipment. They opened up gates to flood the rice fields so future crops would fail and made off with any food and ammunition they could carry. Local slaves, knowing this was the best time to leave, followed the troops by the hundreds. Even Harriet was shocked at their numbers. Because it appeared that there were not enough boats to carry all the fugitives to safety, some began to panic. To calm the crowds, Harriet began to

Company E, Fourth Colored Infantry, at Fort Lincoln

Attack on Fort Wagner, South Carolina. The Colored Infantry was commanded by Robert Gould Shaw, who was killed in action in South Carolina.

sing. Soon others along the riverbank joined in. By the end of the raid, the gunboats were filled with the escaping slaves and about eight hundred people were safely delivered to freedom.

Afterwards, Northern reports of a "black woman Moses" leading the raid circulated through the papers. It was a huge success.

The remainder of the war found Tubman spending much of her time nursing troops back to good health. Harriet also tried to help newly freed blacks return to a normal life, focusing her efforts on starting schools for free blacks. She also witnessed the Fifty-fourth Massachusetts regiment's famous attack on Battery Wagner near Charleston, South Carolina. This all-black regiment was lead by white Colonel Robert Gould Shaw. Though the attack was unsuccessful, the brave troops of the Fifty-fourth proved that African American soldiers deserved a place on the battlefield. In recent years, the Fifty-fourth was celebrated in the movie *Glory*.

Harriet followed Colonel James Montgomery's men to Florida as part of a force of combined white and black regiments, and she produced medicines made from local herbs to help heal the soldiers wounded in battle. At the end of the war, Harriet was working as a nurse in Fortress Monroe, Virginia, taking care of wounded black soldiers.

CHAPTER 10
LIFE AFTER THE CIVIL WAR

Two years after the Civil War ended, Harriet Tubman received word that John Tubman, her former husband, had died. Around the same time she met Nelson Davis, a black war veteran. She and Davis married two years later.

From most accounts, Nelson and Harriet spent a happy twenty years together. Although he still suffered from bronchial problems dating back to the war, they seemed to complement each other well. Nelson helped rebuild their home in Auburn, New York, after a fire in 1886; the rebuilt brick house still stands today.

Harriet Tubman's life after the war may have seemed placid in comparison to her work in the Underground Railroad and as a spy, but she always had battles to fight. The first was getting back pay from the U.S. Army. Though she gave three years of service to the army, and even with Union officers vouching for her incredible work, she still only was paid about $200. She continued to fight for her pension, and finally, about thirty years after the end of the war, the government agreed to pay her $20 per month.

It is reported that Harriet used most of the money the government paid her during the Civil War to build a laundry house to help provide jobs for freedwomen. Of course, this was normal for Harriet Tubman. Money was always difficult for her to hold onto because she was usually donating whatever she had to her church, to schools for newly free black children, and to other causes, including the fight for the right of women to vote.

Tubman already had some property set aside in Auburn, New York, that she had acquired before the Civil War. Noticing that the land next door already had two large buildings, one brick and one frame (along with numerous outbuildings and sheds), Tubman decided it was time to expand her holdings.

In 1896 she purchased this additional 25 acres (10 hectares) of property. Her intention was to use the land to establish a "home for the aged." Harriet was already about seventy years old herself, but that didn't stop her. She contacted the elders at the AME Zion Church and informed them of her plans; they helped secure additional money for the purchase.

In a few years, though, the uncertainty of her income made Harriet rethink her plan. At one point she didn't have enough money to pay the taxes on her land and had to sell off some of her cows just to raise the funds she needed.

By 1903, Harriet was almost eighty years old. She decided to donate the property to the AME Zion Church, but only if they let her hold the deed and continue to keep working on her home for the aged. Within five years, there were enough funds to staff the home and outfit it for residents. (Of course, some were living there already!) The opening celebration on June 23, 1908, was probably one of Harriet's happiest days, and she celebrated by sharing amazing stories from her life with the crowds assembled.

By 1911, Harriet Tubman's long life was coming to a close. She moved out of her own house and into the Home for the Aged she'd helped create. Two years later, feeling that her time was drawing near, she told her friends and family that she knew she would die soon. She was very calm—even joining in the hymns sung by her bedside when she had the strength. Harriet Tubman passed away peacefully on the night of March 10, 1913. She was almost ninety-three years old. Harriet was buried with military honors in the Fort Hill Cemetery in Auburn.

THE HARRIET TUBMAN HOME FOR THE AGED

The African Methodist Episcopal Zion Church has preserved a 26-acre (10-ha) site in New York dedicated to the later life and work of Harriet Tubman. The church was able to preserve and restore the building that housed the Harriet Tubman Home for the Aged after the city ordered it demolished in 1944. Today the home houses a museum and is open for tours throughout the year (map reference 12).

Above: Harriet Tubman led many slaves—including her parents—to freedom through the Underground Railroad.

Left: Harriet Tubman in about 1910 when she had become an old woman

CHAPTER 11
HARRIET TUBMAN'S LEGACY

The courage and hard work of heroes like Harriet Tubman did much to improve the lives of African Americans, yet things did not immediately get easier for emancipated slaves. Immediately after the war, during the time now known as Reconstruction, Southern blacks found themselves free and with expanded opportunities to own property, start businesses, and serve in elected offices. Some blacks took advantage of these opportunities, but others— lacking the education and wealth of whites—could not.

Soon, some of the opportunities offered to former slaves started to disappear. Southern whites, bitter over the lost war and hardened by generations of racism, created a social and legal system to oppress African Americans. In about 1890, Southern states started to pass "Jim Crow laws," legislation that reversed the civil rights gains that blacks had made during Reconstruction and segregated whites and blacks into separate societies. At the same time, the white supremacist Ku Klux Klan grew in popularity and power; the secret fraternal organization carried out countless acts of violence against blacks. Southern blacks soon found themselves with lives and prospects not much better than their enslaved ancestors.

Following the example set by Harriet Tubman in an earlier generation, many blacks chose to escape the South in the early twentieth century, migrating north to better economic and educational opportunities. By the 1950s, African Americans, fighting for a better life, spawned a full-blown civil rights movement. Legal battles by the National Association for the Advancement of Colored People led to overturning Jim Crow laws and ending segregation in the South. One of the heroes of the movement was a black woman named Rosa Parks, who refused to give up her seat to a white man on a bus in Montgomery, Alabama; she was arrested. National civil rights leaders such as Dr. Martin Luther King, Jr., jumped to her aid and protests followed. Her case went all the way to the United States Supreme Court, where the court ruled that segregated bus service was unconstitutional. No doubt that Harriet Tubman would have been proud of Parks's protest in the face of unfair treatment.

African Americans have made great strides, thanks to the civil rights movement, but many problems related to racial inequality remain. Black U.S. citizens still earn less money, on average, than white citizens, and they suffer from higher levels of unemployment and poverty. Racial discrimination and violence directed against people just because of the color of their skin still exist in the United States. We can still hope that African Americans' journey to full freedom and equality—a journey first embarked upon by escaping slaves like Harriet Tubman—will finally be complete in the not-too-distant future.

Below: **Martin Luther King, Jr., listens at a meeting of the Southern Christian Leadership Conference, at a restaurant in Atlanta. The SCLC is a civil rights organization formed by Martin Luther King, Jr., after the success of the Montgomery bus boycott.**

Inset: **Civil rights leaders, including Martin Luther King, Jr., surrounded by crowds carrying signs on August 28, 1963**

Place to Visit and Research

Many sites crucial to Harriet Tubman and the Underground Railroad can be researched on line or visited. Below is a list in alphabetical order of some of those historic sites, parks, museums, and houses, along with their addresses, telephone numbers, Web sites. Places described in the sidebars are shown on the map on pages 58–59 with green dots. The red dots refer to other places important to the Underground Railroad.

1 Amistad America
746 Chapel Street, Suite 300, New Haven, CT 06510. (203) 495-1839. www.amistadamerica.org
See page 19.

2 Bethel African Methodist Episcopal Church
119 North Tenth Street, Reading, PA 19610. (570) 215-0001. www.cr.nps.gov/nr/travel/underground/pa3.htm. See page 26.

3 Boston African-American Historic Site
14 Beacon Stree, Suite 503, Boston, MA 02108. (617) 742-5415. www.nps.gov/boaf/about.htm
By 1800, Boston had one of the largest communities of free African Americans in North America.

4 Bucktown Village Store
4303 Bucktown Road Cambridge, MD. (410) 228-7650.
This store was the site of the accident that led to Tubman's injuries and future blackouts. It is open today to tourists, who are welcomed by the present owners.

5 Dorchester (Maryland) County Department of Tourism
2 Rose Hill Place, Cambridge, Maryland 21613. (410) 228-1000. www.tourdorchester.org
Harriet's home county was the starting place of her journey to freedom.

6 The Eli Whitney Museum
915 Whitney Avenue, Hamden, CT 06517-4036. (203) 777-1833 www.eliwhitney.org.
See page 15.

7 Fort Sumter National Monument
1214 Middle Street, Sullivan's Island, SC 29482. (843) 883-3123. www.nps.gov/fosu. See page 47.

8 Frederick Douglass National Historic Site
1411 W Street SE, Washington, DC 20020. (202) 426-5961. www.nps.gov/frdo/index.htm.
See page 21.

9 Harpers Ferry National Historic Park
P.O. Box 65, Harpers Ferry, West Virginia 25425. (304) 535-6298. www.nps.gov/hafe/home.htm.
See page 45.

10 Harriet Beecher Stowe Center
77 Forest Street, Hartford, CT 06105. (860) 522-9258. www.harrietbeecherstowecenter.org

11 Harriet Beecher Stowe House
2950 Gilbert Avenue, Cincinnati, OH 45214. (513) 632-5100. www.ohiohistory.org/places/stowe.
See page 35.
Harriet Beecher Stowe's home and her writings are on view to inspire others interested in pursuing social justice.

12 The Harriet Tubman Home
180 South Street Auburn, NY 13201. (315) 252-2081. www.nyhistory.com/harriettubman/home.htm. See page 53.

13 Harriet Tubman Museum & Learning Center
424 Race Street, Cambridge, MD 21613. (410) 228-0401. See page 11.

14 Hubbard House Underground Railroad Museum
P.O. Box 2666, Ashtabula, OH 44005-2666. (440) 964-8168. www.hubbardhouseugrrmuseum.org
Colonel William Hubbard's house near the shores of Lake Erie was one of the last stops that escaping slaves made before crossing the border into Canada.

15 John Brown State Historic Site
10th and Main Street, Osawatomie, KS 66064. (913) 755-4384. xwww.kshs.org/places/johnbrown.
See page 45.

16 John Brown's Farm State Historic Site
John Brown Road, Lake Placid, NY 12946. (518) 523-3900. nysparks.state.ny.us/sites/info.asp?siteID=12.
See page 45.

17 John P. Parker House
300 Front Street, Ripley, OH 45167. (937) 392-4188. www.johnparkerhouse.org

Once a slave, John Parker was a conductor on the Underground Railroad.

18 John Rankin House

6152 Rankin Road, Ripley, OH 45167. (937) 392-1627. www.ripleyohio.net/rankin.htm. See pages 40 and 41.

19 The Johnson House Historic Site

6306 Germantown Avenue, Philadelphia, PA 19144 (215) 438-1768. www.johnsonhouse.org. See page 27.

20 Kelton House Museum and Garden

586 East Town Street, Columbus, OH 43215. (614) 464-2022. www.keltonhouse.com/index.html
The Kelton House is a preserved station on the Underground Railroad.

21 The LeMoyne House

49 East Maiden Street, Washington, PA 15301. (724) 225-6740. www.wchspa.org/html/house.htm
Dr. Francis Julius LeMoyne and his entire family were active in the Underground Railroad. Their home is a National Historic Landmark and museum and is open for tours throughout the year.

22 Levi Coffin House

113 U.S. 27 North, Fountain City, IN 47341. (765) 847-2432. www.waynet.org/nonprofit/coffin.htm. See pages 39–40.

23 The Milton House

18 South Janesville Street, Milton, WI 53563. (608) 868-7772. www.miltonhouse.org. See page 41.

24 Motherland Connexions Underground Railroad Tours

P.O. Box 176 Bridge Street Station, Niagara Falls, NY 14305. (716) 282-1028. www.motherlandconnextions.com/tours.html
On these guided package tours of historic sites in western New York and Ontario, participants can visit many of the places frequented by Harriet Tubman as she guided escaped slaves to freedom on the Underground Railroad.

25 The National Archives Experience

700 Constitution Avenue NW, Washington, DC 20408 (866) 272-6272. www.archives.gov/national_archives_experience. See page 49.

26 The Newton History Museum at the Jackson Homestead

527 Washington Street, Newton, MA 02458. (617) 796-1450. www.ci.newton.ma.us/jackson/default.asp
This was a stop on the Underground Railroad; William Jackson, who lived here from 1820 to 1855, was an active abolitionist.

27 Rokeby Museum

4334 Route 7, Ferrisburgh, VT 05456. (802) 877-3406. www.rokeby.org/home.html.
This historic site preserves the home of the Robinson family, Quaker abolitionists and stationmasters on the Underground Railroad in the 1830s and 1840s.

28 Spring Hill Historic Home

1401 Spring Hill Lane NE, Massillon, OH 44646. (330) 833-6749. www.massillonproud.com/springhill See page 23.

29 Underground Railroad Museum

P.O. Box 47, 121 High Street, Flushing, Ohio 43977. (740) 968-2080. www.ugrrf.org.
This museum maintains an extensive collection of artifacts, books, and other Underground Railroad-related items for display.

30 The Village of Mount Pleasant, Ohio

(800) 752-2631 or (740) 769-2893. users.1st.net/gudzent.
This small community, with a preserved historic district, had a strong abolitionist Quaker population, and the entire town served as a large station on the Underground Railroad.

WA

MT

ND

OR

ID

SD

WY

NE

NV

UT

CO

CA

AZ

NM

TX

MEXICO

This map shows the location of the places identified on pages 56–57.
Those places indicated in green dots are also mentioned in sidebars.

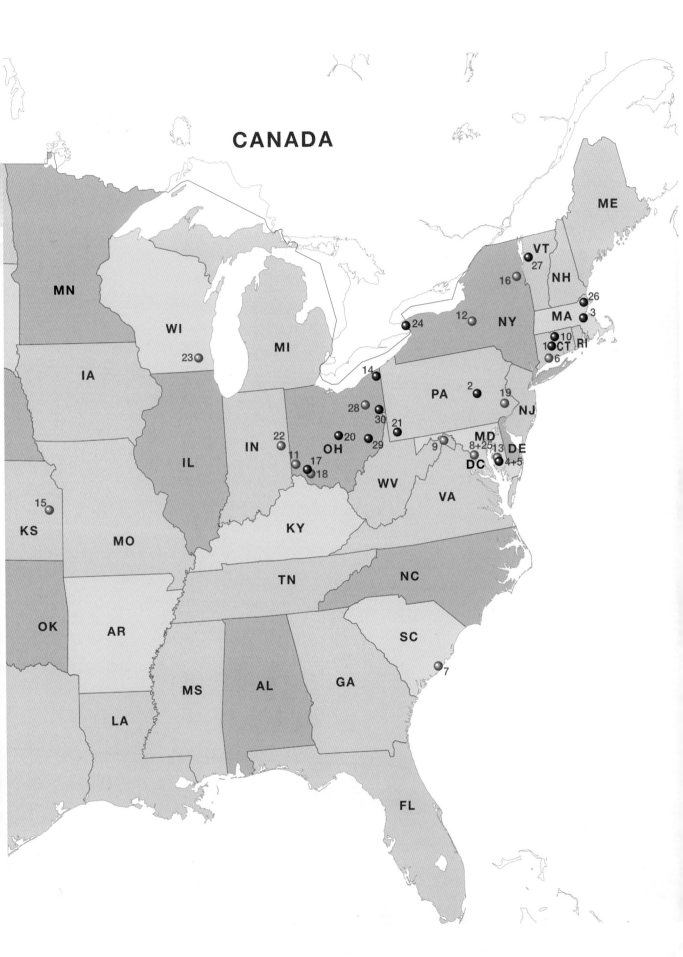

Time Line

1530s
Spanish ships bring the first slaves from Africa to North America.

1619
First slaves arrive in Jamestown.

1776
The colonies declare independence from Great Britain. Black slaves fight alongside whites during the war.

1831
Nat Turner slave rebellion.

1839
Amistad rebellion and famous court case.

1818
Frederick Douglass born.

1820
Harriet Tubman born around this time (exact date unknown) in Dorchester County, Maryland. Her given name is Araminta Ross.

1832
Harriet suffers head injury around this time, resulting in occasional blackouts for the rest of her life.

1840
Harriet's father is freed.

1844
Harriet marries John Tubman, local freeman.

1840s
First mention of the phrase "Underground Railroad" is seen in printed pamphlets and articles.

1849
Harriet escapes to Philadelphia after her owner, Edward Brodess, dies.

1850
Harriet returns to Dorchester County to lead the first group of slaves to freedom. Fugitive Slave Act passes as an attempt to hold the Union together.

1857
Harriet Tubman brings her parents to safety and freedom in St. Catherines, Ontario, Canada.

1858
Harriet meets abolitionist John Brown.

1859
John Brown leads unsuccessful raid on Harper's Ferry, Virginia; he is captured, convicted of treason and murder, and executed.

1860
Harriet goes back to Maryland on her last rescue mission for the Underground Railroad

1861
Civil War begins after Confederate troops in South Carolina fire on Fort Sumter

1862
Harriet works as a nurse for the Union in South Carolina. Abraham Lincoln announces Emancipation Proclamation, freeing all slaves in Confederate states on January 1, 1863.

1863
Harriet Tubman works as a scout and a spy and helps plan and lead a Union raid on Confederate posts in South Carolina.

1865
Civil War ends; Abraham Lincoln is assassinated.

1867
Harriet's former husband, John Tubman, dies in Dorchester County, Maryland.

1869
Harriet marries Nelson Davis, a former soldier and black veteran of the Civil War.

1888
Harriet's husband Nelson Davis dies.

1895
Harriet purchases 25 acres (10 ha) of land that borders her property in Auburn, New York.

1903
Harriet helps found Home for the Aged.

1913
Harriet Tubman dies in New York.

Glossary

Abolitionist
A person, black or white, who was opposed to slavery and worked to abolish it.

Bounty
A reward paid for the capture and return of escaped slaves to their owners.

Bounty hunter
A person who made his living tracking, capturing, and returning escaped slaves.

Compromise of 1850
Five separate bills passed by the U.S. Congress that attempted to stop the growing rift between Northern and Southern states over the issue of slavery.

Conductor
A conductor was someone who, like Harriet Tubman, led slaves through sections of the Underground Railroad to safe quarters. Each conductor might have stayed with a group for a short time or over an entire journey.

Emancipation Proclamation
A presidential decree announced by Abraham Lincoln on September 22, 1862, that freed all slaves in the rebelling Confederates states on January 1, 1863.

Fugitive slave
A person who escaped slavery and was considered a criminal by the laws of the period.

Fugitive Slave Act
A law passed as part of the Compromise of 1850 that required law enforcement officials in all states to arrest anyone suspected of being an escaped slave. In addition, the act required stiff penalties for anybody providing food or shelter to an escaped slave.

Indentured servant
A person bound by an indenture (a contract) to work for another person for a specific period of time, usually for four to seven years, in return for specified benefits. The benefits usually included transportation to the New World and food and shelter while under contract.

Mason-Dixon Line
Charles Mason and Jeremiah Dixon surveyed a border between Pennsylvania and Maryland in the 1760s. It came to stand as a dividing line between free and slave states and North and South. At least symbolically, crossing the line was an important step for an escaping slave.

Missouri Compromise An agreement engineered in 1820 by Kentucky Congressman Henry Clay to allow Missouri to enter the Union as a slave state while Maine was granted statehood as a free state.

Opium
An addictive, narcotic (sleep-inducing) drug made from the juice of the opium poppy.

Seminary
A college that trains people to be ministers, priests, or rabbis.

Station
Any place a fugitive slave could rest and be safe from pursuers. Each station was secured by a person known as a stationmaster. A station often wasn't fancy—it could be a cave, a cellar, or a barn. Some stations were even moving objects, such as a horse-drawn wagon or an actual railroad car.

Slave
A person who was owned by another person as property and had to work for that individual without pay. Slaves had no legal rights, could be bought and sold, and their lives and actions were completely controlled by their owners.

Underground Railroad
The complete web of trails, safe houses, stations, and routes to freedom in the North used by escaping slaves from the late 1700s until 1865. In some places, like Philadelphia and southern Ohio, the Underground Railroad was very organized. In other places, and kindly people who sympathized with escaping slaves did what they could to help them on the spot.

Further Resources

Books

Bradford, Sarah, *Harriet Tubman: The Moses of Her People*, New York: Citadel Press, 1974

Clinton, Catherine, *Harriet Tubman: The Road to Freedom*, New York: Little, Brown, 2004

Davis, Kenneth, C., *Don't Know Much About The Civil War: Everything You Need to Know About America's Greatest Conflict, But Never Learned*, New York: Perennial, 1999

Davis, William C. *Look Away! A History of the Confederate States of America*, New York: The Free Press, 2002

DeRamus, Betty, *Forbidden Fruit: Love Stories from the Underground Railroad*, New York: Atria Books, 2005

Douglass, Frederick, *Narrative of the Life of Frederick Douglass: An American Slave, written by Himself*, New Haven, CT: Yale University Press, 2001.

Du Bois, W. E. B., *John Brown*, New York: Modern Library Classics (reprint edition), 2001

Hawke, David Freeman, *Everyday Life in Early America*, New York: Perennial, 2003

Hendrick, George and Willene (eds.), *Fleeing For Freedom: Stories of the Underground Railroad As Told by Levi Coffin and William Still*, Chicago: Ivan R. Dee Publishing, 2004

Larson, Kate Clifford, *Bound for the Promised Land: Harriet Tubman, Portrait of an American Hero*, New York: Ballantine, 2004

Levine, Ellen, *If You Traveled on the Underground Railroad*, New York: Scholastic, 1993.

Tobin, Jacqueline L. and Raymond D. Dobard, *Hidden in Plain View: A Secret Story of Quilts and the Underground Railroad*, New York: Anchor Books, 2000

Ward, Geoffrey C., with Ken Burns and Ric Burns. *The Civil War: An Illustrated History*, New York: Borzoi Books, 1990

Web Sites

Aboard the Underground Railroad: A National Register Travel Itinerary
www.cr.nps.gov/nr/travel/underground/ugrrhome.htm

Africans In America
www.pbs.org/wgbh/aia/home.html

AmericanCivilWar.com
www.americancivilwar.com

Amistad America
www.amistadamerica.org/

The Civil War Home Page
www.civil-war.net

CivilWarTraveler.com
www.civilwartraveler.com

Harriet Tubman.com
www.harriettubman.com/index.html

Harriet Tubman & The Underground Railroad for Children
www2.lhric.org/pocantico/tubman/tubman.html

Harriet Tubman Biography
www.harriettubmanbiography.com

National Geographic Presents: The Underground Railroad
www.nationalgeographic.com/railroad/index.html

National Underground Railroad Network to Freedom
www.cr.nps.gov/ugrr

New York History Net: The Life of Harriet Tubman
www.nyhistory.com/harriettubman/life.htm

Pathways to Freedom: Maryland and the Underground Railroad
pathways.thinkport.org/flash_home.cfm

Voices from the Days of Slavery: Former Slaves Tell Their Stories
lcweb2.loc.gov/ammem/collections/voices

Index

Bold numbers indicate illustrations.